Cinema Muto

CRAB ORCHARD SERIES IN POETRY

Open Competition Award

CINEMA MUTO

Jesse Lee Kercheval

Crab Orchard Review

&

Southern Illinois University Press

CARBONDALE

12   11   10   09   4   3   2   1

The Crab Orchard Series in Poetry is a joint publishing venture of Southern
Illinois University Press and *Crab Orchard Review*. This series has been made
possible by the generous support of the Office of the President of Southern
Illinois University and the Office of the Vice Chancellor for Academic Affairs
and Provost at Southern Illinois University Carbondale.

Crab Orchard Series in Poetry Editor: Jon Tribble
Open Competition Award Judge for 2008: David Wojahn

Library of Congress Cataloging-in-Publication Data
Kercheval, Jesse Lee.
Cinema muto / Jesse Lee Kercheval.
p. cm. — (Crab Orchard series in poetry)
Includes bibliographical references.
ISBN-13: 978-0-8093-2895-6 (alk. paper)
ISBN-10: 0-8093-2895-x (alk. paper)
I. Title.
PS3561.E558C56 2009
811'.54—dc22

2008032845

Printed on recycled paper. ♻
The paper used in this publication meets the minimum requirements
of American National Standard for Information Sciences—Permanence of
Paper for Printed Library Materials, ANSI Z39.48-1992. ♾

FOR DAN

Contents

{ ACT III }

Acknowledgments

I would like to acknowledge with gratitude the magazines in which the following poems first appeared:

American Literary Review—"Germinal"

Ascent—"Ein Werktag"

The Atlanta Review—"Goodnight Silents"

Chelsea—"Last year, you were in Italy" and *"L'Hirondelle et la Mesange"*

The Crab Orchard Review—"Imagine God as a Camera," "The Adventures of Billy," and *"Voyage Autour D'Une Etoile"*

The Denver Quarterly—"La Vocation D'André Carel: The Vocation of André Carel"

5 AM—"Visage D'Enfants" and *"Kohitsuji: The Lamb"*

THE DIAGRAM—"silent night" and "The Projector"

Epoch—"Byzantium"

Hotel Amerika—"The Dark That Is Not Sleeping" and "Film Upon Film"

The Missouri Review—"Saving Silence" and *"Kurutta Ippeiji*: A Page of Madness"

New American Writing—"Tusalava"

Pleiades—"Fragments from *Le Mogli e le Arance*: Wives and Oranges"

Poetry East—"My Husband—Lover of Silent Movies—Attends *Le Giornate del Cinema Muto*"

Poetry Northwest—"Bang" and "Familiarity, My Husband"

Prairie Schooner—"This is not a silent movie—there is music," "Before the Movie," and "film history as train wreck"

The Salt River Review—"Le Carnard, c. 1925?"

Sentence: A Journal of Prose Poetics—"Italy, October"

The Southern Review—"I Due Signi Ad Occhi Aperti: Two Dreams with Eyes Wide Open" and "The Acting Career of Charles H. West Considered as Bad Karma"

Willow Springs—"D. W. Griffith, December, 1911" and "from the last century"

"Mosjoukine in Exile" and "film history as train wreck" appeared in the limited edition, letter press chapbook *film history as train wreck* (New York: Center for Book Arts, 2006).

My warmest thanks to *Le Giornate del Cinema Muto* for making these poems possible. I also want to thank the Corporation of Yaddo, the Graduate School Research Committee of the University of Wisconsin, and Sally Mead Hands for their generous support.

ACT I

Saving Silence

"In an astonishingly short time—1895 to 1927, little more than thirty years—
the silent cinema evolved into a unique, integral and highly sophisticated
expressive form, and then, over night became extinct."
                    —David Robinson, foreword to *Silent Cinema, An Introduction*

Isn't that the way of things—
where is Carthage now,
the dodo? In archives
in America, Japan & Russia
there are as many feet
of nitrate film dissolving
as there are bones
in the catacombs of Paris.
Of one hundred & fifty thousand
silent films, eighty percent
are as lost to us
as the dust our grand-
parents returned to.
So why do I care? Because
my mother was deaf,
because I am tired after years
of talk-talk-talking.
Because as a child, I once
rode the elevator
to the top of the Eiffel Tower
where, like God,
I looked down &
saw the whole world
at my feet—
rendered not motionless,
but silent.

My Husband—Lover of Silent Movies—
Attends *Le Giornate del Cinema Muto*

The words start to fade,
even before he arrives
at the silent film festival.
On take-off from O'Hare
his eustachian tubes
fill & never quite clear,
sound drowning
in his inner ear.
Once in Sacile,
not knowing Italian,
he is reduced
to the same state
as the family dog,
listening intently,
head cocked to one side,
understanding
only his name.
The name on the tag
the young assistant hangs
around his neck
at the *Teatro Zancanaro*
before the lights go out
& the screen is filled w/
deliberate silence,
w/ the black & white
gestures of a lost
world. Then he belongs,
then he can hear
all the words
that are not being spoken.

The Adventures of Billy

"When young Billy witnesses two tramps killing a robbery victim, they decide
Billy must be killed and lock him in a shed."

—*The Griffith Project: Volume V*

On the screen
an orphan boy gestures
to a dog w/
a wild flapping
of his arms.
Get help!
his splayed fingers
say. *Go now,*
is the shape his lips make.
The dog hears.

We do too—
though no one is talking
we hear the world
with keen new ears
as if we were rat terriers.
We lean forward
in our red velvet seats,
ready to rescue Billy ourselves—
from the fire the tramps set,
from 1911,
from the fate of a child star
working for D. W. Griffith.

We know
what the audience then
could not know—

that two world wars
are coming,
that Billy is a girl
named Edna Foster,
that for Griffith
the world would stop
in 1927
with the coming
of sound.

But for now,
we know no more
than Griffith lets us—
will the dog take the message
to his master? Will
the racing car
reach the burning shed
in time? This must
be how God
views the living—
knowing how each
life ends
but still caught up
in the story.

silent night

now there is not exactly
silence, there will be piano
& the sound of people
coughing in the dark
—do not be afraid—
the ensuing hour will be
luminous & everything
will have the need to burn
but I swear it will be *there*
as it is in here: dogs swimming
in the rivers, rivers full of boys—
though because every movie
has to have a story
someone's life or heart
will be at risk—
so sit up straight &
be prepared
for a unifying light.

Kurutta Ippeiji: A Page of Madness

This experimental silent film was thought lost for fifty years until the director
Teinosuke "Kinugasa himself rediscovered it in his garden shed."

—*Le Giornate del Cinema Muto catalogue*

An old man takes a job
as a janitor at an asylum
to be near his wife
who failed to drown herself
after drowning their infant son—
tiny squalling bundle.

This is Japan. The year 1926.

His wife lies on the floor
of her cell on her futon.
Her kimono disordered—
her hair a disgrace.
Her arms rise from her sides
as she sleeps, her hands open,
begging for forgiveness.
Or is she dreaming
of the moment
she let her baby go?

In the next cell, a young woman
dances day and night
without stopping, leaving bare
bloody footprints across
the concrete floor. She is a goddess
but only she knows it.
If the old man asked her—
she would give him back his son.

But the old man sees
only a mad girl
who once—he's been told—
danced the May Dance
for Crown Prince Hirohito,
then found she couldn't stop.

The old man unlocks his wife's cell
with a key he has stolen
from the desk of the director,
in his other hand are sweets.
Their daughter, he tells her,
their only daughter,
has met a young man
who's asked her to marry,
to move north with him
to his home in far Hokkaido,
that wild frontier island.

When asked, their daughter
told this young man
her mother died giving birth
to a stillborn baby brother.
She understands clearly
if he knew where her mother was—
what she was—
even a boy from Hokkaido
would not take her home.

Your daughter, says the old man.
Remember you have a daughter.
And the wife does—
remembers the young hands
that kept her from the river,
from following
the same arc as her baby.

If her daughter loved her,
she would not have stopped her.
Even now, years later, she can feel
ten ugly bruises
left by her daughter's long strong fingers.
Even now, years later,
she still suffers with this living
her selfish daughter gave her.

Come, the old man tells his wife.
Your children need you.
Forgetting, at that moment,
only one is still alive.
He uses sweets to lure his wife
from her cell, down
the long stone hallway.
If only she would come home,
the old man keeps on thinking—
*our daughter could have children
without moving to Hokkaido.*
Children to replace the one
lost to the spring's cold
rushing water.

He takes his wife's pale hand
and leads her past the dancer,
who has paused for a moment
to rearrange her hair
in a mirror that is not there.
They make it to the front door.
He still has the candies and his wife
—who, as a girl, was famous
for her sweet tooth—clearly wants them.
He won the sweets, he tells her,
this morning at the street fair.
This, he remarks, *is our lucky day.*

Outside, in the dark night,
a dog is barking and his wife
is frightened—she always
has been frightened.
Even before this place,
even before her children
began crying every night.

She is crying now
as she pulls her hand from her husband's,
runs back down the hall
to her cell, throws herself, sobbing,
into the cold nothing that awaits her.
No daughter, nosey no good,
to stop her now.

The old man goes home,
falls to the floor exhausted,
sweets still in his hand.
He hears a girl dance
the May Dance
in a warm spring far away
and dreams, instead of candies,
he won masks at the street fair—
smooth white faces
with smiling, wide red mouths.
In his sleep, he hands the masks
out to the mad ones
as he mops slowly
past their cells.

One by one the mad
put on new faces
and become as they should
have always been—
smiling, happy.

They laugh gently, stepping
freely from their cells—
children
come home at last
to their mothers,
fathers.

His wife is smiling too.
White world, red life,
the goddess says,
still dancing,
and hands the wife a pillow
that in an instant
becomes a smiling baby.

Or did I dream
this ending? Fall asleep
like the old man and dream
the end I wanted—
because I also had a mother
who happened to go mad,
though I failed
to catch her
when she threw herself away.
Because I too lost a child—
though she fell
from my womb and not my hands,
leaving the water
that was me
behind.

Still, I remember
the end so vividly—
how in the silver light,
the dancing woman

joined hands
with the old man and his wife,
the red-lipped inmates
to form a perfect circle.
And the circle, I saw clearly,
was the world
and even I—and even you—
were there.

Last year, you were in Italy

alone, eating octopus,
boiled pink and lovely as a rose.
I was home, a woman
with a baby carriage
in her garage, popsicles
in five fruit flavors
in the freezer of her fridge,
who could, without a thought,
have her only male cat fixed.

On Friday, you wrote, *I am
going to Pordenone. For lunch
had crustini and porcini.*
At home, what I ate was shoes,
what I drank was raw regret.
*If that woman continues
to go on like that*, I said
as if someone else
was crying, *I may have
to leave the room.*

The Dark That Is Not Sleeping

movies + dreams (handwritten)

In the dark that is the living room
a girl might ask   *What is a movie?*
just to hear her sister say   *A world you walk into*
just to hear her father say   *A house inside our house*
only to hear her mother say   *Little girl*

you should be in bed—
But in bed is not asleep

Later a woman who is still awake
and who happens to be me asks   *Why me, God?*
of her pillow   her alarm clock,   her
short wave radio tuned to endless BBC. Only the announcer
answers, promising

the end of the world   news

So I go into my living room to watch a movie
          world I walk into
          house inside my house
          dream I rent or buy

Start a silent film—*no dialogue or loud explosions*—
just an upright
someone added as a sound track
knowing   how rare
insomniac pianists are
as roommates or   as lovers.

I fall asleep   and dream,
writing intertitles in place of ones
my shut eyes   cannot read

As if rehearsing sleep is what sleep needs
sleep begins to come
and dreams   different
from the movies

Then one night   I fall asleep in bed
just thinking of a movie. Then the next night too
so I have to watch my movies

sitting-up-wide-awake the way   my father
used to do

But sometimes   I confess   I make a pot of coffee
to stay *awake*
to remind myself how
one-reeler *short short short*   this life is
how much time   we waste in sleeping

If dreams *are* a waste
and not—
          the world we walk into
the house inside our house
          the place we wait, eyes wide shut

as silent,

God   approaches

Familiarity, My Husband

One morning in
the small Italian town
where we are staying,
you discover the church door open.
Inside we find the body
of Saint Gregory,
his bones dressed
in embroidered satin
& we can't help comparing him
to other the saints
we've seen in our travels:
Santa Lucia with her heap
of eyeglasses in Venice,
Mother Cabrini marooned
in the upper reaches of Manhattan,
St. Boniface, unfamous
apostle to the Germans.

Like the explorer
Sir Richard Burton—
we take ourselves with us
everywhere we go.
He traveled
all five continents,
learned a hundred languages.
By the time he wrote
his final book on Iceland
every rock he saw
was the shadow of a dozen others,
every word
had ten synonyms
in his cacophony of language.

In the end,
no one could understand
a thing he said.
—not his most ardent reader.
—not his wife Isabel who rarely traveled.

No one except God. One can always
hope for God.

&—I count my blessings—
I have you.

At least for this life;
at least for now.

Voyage Autour D'Une Etoile

"An old astronomer has long adored a star. He has only one desire—to approach it and declare his passion. But how shall he achieve this? Watching children playing with soap bubbles gives him an idea."

—*Le Giornate del Cinema Muto catalogue*

An old astronomer floats
into the sky
inside a giant bubble.
Should we take this as a sign
of man's desire
to draw nearer
to the heavens,
of his desire
to come closer, God,
to you?

Or is this merely base
desire? The stars
busty, long-haired beauties
in a harem;
the moon
the jealous sultan of the sky
who tosses
the old astronomer
from the palace
of the heavens.

Pathé filmed this *Voyage*
twice, in 1906 &
again in 1907—
a common practice
in those days

when the negative
wore out
from making prints.

In the first, the astronomer,
falling to earth,
is impaled
on a lightning rod.
A death not unlike
the sad pagan end
of Icarus.

In the remake,
the astronomer
falls with a harmless
splash into his washtub
full of bubbles.

I confess,
coming clean
as an end
seems a better
thing to hope for.
I bathe every morning, God—
can I consider
myself cleansed?

Kohitsuji: The Lamb

This is what happens:
Toshihiko, our hero, is tied up
by a villain known as The Wolf,
& tossed off a cliff
only to land alive
at the bottom,
miraculously unbound,
on a motherlode of gold.

This is a man who
had his heart broken
by a famous courtesan,
a man who was found
near death by a young
shepherdess who nursed him
back to health.

After his fall, Toshihiko
becomes *The King of Gold*.
He spurns the now attentive
courtesan & marries
his devoted shepherdess.

Could I have this life, please?

But minus the heartbreak,
the fall from great heights.

Just give me the gold
&
let me be the lamb.

Italy, October

To be here is to be where fruit you have never seen before grows on equally strange trees. The fruit is not, as you first thought, oranges, though it is orange in color. Nor is it a tangerine or some strangely colored apple. Then you see it in the market, each soft fruit cradled in its own nest of woven plastic. *Cachi*, the sign reads, *200 lire.* You hold out a palm of silver, and let the cashier pick warm coins from your waiting hand. Then she wraps your *cachi* in white paper like a present, which you carry to your hotel, hoping *cachi* can be safely eaten raw.

In your room, you slice it open, lift the *cachi* to your lips and find it sweeter than any fruit you've ever tasted, half watermelon, half pressed roses. Only when you've finished, do you think to look up *cachi* in your pocket Italian dictionary which says it means *persimmon.* And you remember as a child picking a persimmon at a friend's house, then leaving it all afternoon in your mother's stand-up freezer. Still, when you bit the unripe fruit, your mouth drew up in a pucker from which you—silent person that you are—never did recover. Until today in Sacile when you took a bite of strange fruit.

Now, who knows?   You may speak in tongues.

Ein Werktag

"[This 1931 Swiss film] depicts human destinies caught up in the realities of life.
A truck driver . . . and a shop girl . . . face long working hours, exhausting labor,
low salaries, and the constant threat of unemployment."
                                        —*Le Giornate del Cinema Muto catalogue*

do you remember? how despite

the shuttered window
the closed and mended curtains
the smell of mountains   was in every corner

was all the breath there was?
we were without experience   were novices
at love

the mountains!
to smell them in the middle of city
trucks grinding by outside

was to be blessed
though we ached from foot to head
with this love

which was clearly not   *agape*
a man walks this earth
in his tight skin

in rain
and drought   with nothing much
to fear from either

but love
the world's incisor
gnawed us to the bone

still   there were   mountains
beyond the curtain
do you remember?

the smell of snow in every room

Byzantium

Our love is like Byzantium, a place I can hardly imagine,
a place that exists now only as archeology, ruins captured

on the oldest of films, yellowed & crackling, shelved deep
in state-run archives. Somewhere—Berlin?—they have mosaics

from Byzantium—*the golden, the splendid*—stored in
numbered boxes in a stadt museum basement. Somewhere—

the Vatican?—they have religious artifacts, rescued from
the infidels, displayed in dusty, poorly lit glass cases.

To see such things as are left of Byzantium requires
appointments and appointments require letters of introduction.

May I introduce myself to you, Herr Doktor Fuller?

I am your wife, Frau Professor Kercheval. You may kiss my hand—
Door to Byzantium, City of Wonders,

Kiss my hand, my elbow, then later my neck.

I Due Sogni Ad Occhi Aperti: Two Dreams with Eyes Wide Open

"Today almost completely forgotten, between the two World Wars, the writer-director Lucio D'Ambra's name . . . was primarily linked with 'light and polite comedy.'"

—*Le Giornate del Cinema Muto catalogue*

{ I }
The First Dream with Open Eyes

Reginetta, poor girl, has lost
everything in the Messina earthquake
except her caged canary.
She staggers off a train
in Rome, so tired she falls asleep
on the cold stone steps of the church,
San Gregorio al Celio,
her only sweater draped
over the bird's fragile,
fretwork cage.

The last night of the Carnival—
Prince Massimo di Luni
& his bored friends roam the streets
in their tuxedos, singing,
arm in arm, unhooking horses
from cabs with sleeping drivers, pulling
hats over the eyes of other drunken men,
until they come upon Reginetta,
poor sleeping Reginetta,
& her sleeping, covered bird.

The Prince has an idea
he finds clever—they will carry

the girl, still sleeping, to his palace—
& make her a princess for a single,
fleeting day. They do so, ordering the maid
to dress still-sleeping Reginetta
while they change into their own operatic finery.
At first, when she wakes, the girl
is frantic, then Reginetta sees her bird
& decides all the misery of her life before
was the nightmare—that the palace,
with its kind maid & handsome prince,
has always been her home.

The Prince & Princepessa di Luni
marry after a grand procession
through the palace. Even the canary
gets a wife & a golden cage. Then
at dinner, a little powder in her goblet,
& Reginetta's fast asleep. They dress her
in her ragged clothes, take the bird
from his mate & stick him in his old cage.
Then gently, so as not to wake her,
they carry Reginetta to *San Gregorio*
& arrange her on the steps.

{ II }
A Small Interjection Addressed to Lucio D'Ambra, Writer & Director

What part of this abduction,
is "light" or "polite"? Or
(even slightly) "comic"?

{ III }
Life in the World After So Much Dreaming

Reginetta is saved from madness
by the maid from the prince's palace

who finds her on the church steps
& tells her all that happened.
Reginetta finally finds a job at a laundry,
ironing sheets, then one day,
as she is singing in the steamy basement,
a famous impresario hears her
& invites her to sing in his new opera.

So she does. In silent movies, women
either marry well or sing opera—honestly,
there seem to be no other choices,
not even in America where, surely,
opera singers were far less common. Reginetta
becomes an overnight sensation,
& the Prince—who fails to recognize her—
falls deeply in her spell.

{ IV }
The Second Dream with Open Eyes

Reginetta, who despises the Prince
for his treatment of her, plans revenge.
The Prince sends her note after pleading note
telling her how much he loves her,
but she spurns him. Then, one night,
she has his old friends—now hers instead—
drug & carry him to her apartment.
For a single day, she pretends
she loves him, that they are newly married.
Then, just before the consummation,
again, the powder in the wine &
his friends carry the Prince, sleeping,
home to his empty palace.

{ V }

After the Dreams Are Over

My husband says the second dream
was crueler. *Without love*, he says,
all the Prince's wealth means nothing.
Nonsense, I shoot back, the Prince left
Reginetta with less than nothing.
She could have starved for all he cared.
We argue & walk & argue then
we kiss, hard, in the middle of the wet street
as if we might never stop.

{ VI }

My Mother Said All Life's a Dream

Maybe that is why, in spite of everything,
this movie has a happy ending.
Reginetta & the Prince are reconciled
& confess to having loved each other
from the moment they first met.
But the canary, even in the last shot,
sits alone in his tiny, battered cage.
No wife, no aviary
full of fledgling children.

But still, he sings.
But still, he has his dreams.

This is not a silent movie—there is music

& you are the pianist, your breathing,
your slight cough, the sighing of your hair
the only notes I hear. Together, we are naked
in the darkness. Before I prowled the streets
but all that noise meant absolutely nothing.
Lovers said they loved me, shouting sometimes
I was so deaf to their cacophonous emotions
but that only made me lonely no matter
what the language. Without knowing,
I hunted for the liquid music that is you.
Now, I hunger for the movement of your fingers,
the pale almonds of your nails barely seen
in dimness. In between each feature
I pace the lobby   *famished*
until the lights go down.

ACT II

Mosjoukine in Exile

"One of the unassailable giants of silent cinema, Ivan [Mosjoukine]'s
image as the quintessential, unrepressed romantic hero [dominated] pre-
revolutionary Russian cinema. As an émigré in France . . . he triumphantly
renewed his image and career, at least for a while."

—*Le Giornate del Cinema Muto catalogue*

{ 1 }

"[Mosjoukine] was often associated with burning, mesmeric eyes."

the eyes reach through time, distracted, feverish as a child,
as hot in the light of the projector,

as our hearts, our hands, & as alive—*how can he have died, alone,*
a pauper, in 1939?

our eyes—in this theater packed to the last, far seats—mirror Mosjoukine's,
his eyes reflect the over-arching Russian sky.

for now, he is *Michel Strogoff*, secret courier for his czar,
condemned to be blinded by the Khan

for revealing himself, for crying out,
as the Tartars whipped his widowed mother.

sorrow is written in his gaze—
he has failed his duty; he has done his best

& a sort of calm release—he will never see such sadness
in this world again.

will we, I want to ask, *will we—now that Mosjoukine is dead?*
Michel Strogoff begs his mother

not too look away, to be brave enough to let her face
be the last thing that he sees.

tears fill his eyes—water of this life—
as the heated sword, that thread of living fire

weaves across the screen,
then everything falls dark, everything drops down

into the night already there
& in this silent film,

in this world where even blood cannot be red,
a single drop oozes down Mosjoukine's cheek,

a tear-shaped bead of black.

{ 2 }

j'ai deux amours & one of them is paris.

the other is an actor, dead more than sixty years, & forgotten in all the spellings
of his transliterated name. O paris, city where I happened to be born, where
Ivan Mosjoukine, brilliant star, fell far & fast to die destitute, abandoned by his
public, the way he'd already died so memorably in *Kean,* crying out Hamlet's line,
Alexander died, Alexander was buried, Alexander returneth into dust! before he sees
a light brighter than his own &, bowing, leaves the stage

o paris, illuminated city east of everywhere I am, berth of all embarking, port of all
return, street of truffles, bed of sharp remembered pain, on the banks, steep banks,
of the river seine—o paris, enigmatic antidote—o glove thrown down which, *per
bon chance,* climbs my hand again! you who took in Mosjoukine when revolution

swept his world away, though my exile is metaphysical, may I ask the same of you? "Certainly, my pet," paris—or is it Mosjoukine?—replies, "*regardez-vous!*"

I do & see the sun slip behind the sugared dome of sacré coeur, put the prickly sweetness in my pocket to munch for *déjeuner*, then stoop to scrounge the trash as Mosjoukine was said, in the end, to do & in the hush, I pick weeds to use as flowers. in the calm, I find sticks to build a fire. In paris, I do all this in all in paris. city I love as incurably, as irrevocably, as impossibly as I love a man as nearly beautiful

j'ai deux amours, Ivan Mosjoukine, & one of them is you.

{ 3 }

Among *L'Enfant du Carnaval's* "most memorable moments is the superb opening shot: Mosjoukine, in a harlequin's outfit, steals up to a dark curtain that fills the screen and yanks it aside . . . to reveal the vast teeming carnival crowds . . . below."

Never mind that your father was a landowner
& you were destined for the law,

you got off that train
& became a child of the carnival—

the joy of your body nearly unrestrainable,
always acrobat, jester, dancer poised on toe.

So happy
the landlord's daughter smiled at you

you throw yourself backward on the bed
bicycling the air

then roll yourself into a sausage in the comforter, unroll
so fast you blur.

I have never felt as alive
as you look on that screen.

Never once do you go through a gate,
if you can leap the fence.

Never fence without dancing—
dance without the suggestion of a duel.

Arms linked, you move through the carnival.
Arms outstretched, you carry the naked dancer from the room.
Arms open, you beckon to the audience.

It makes me feel I am not *living*
not really
though a dictionary might call it by that name.

Moving, you become a perfect poem.
Moving, you become the very thing
I try to write,   & every day

I fail.

{ 4 }

"Following the 1917 Revolution, the . . . troupe [with Mosjoukine] followed
the Russian cinema's path of emigration to Yalta and thence via Constantinople
to Western Europe."

For no reason   we set fire
to the homemade signs that shouted from the lamp posts:
Coat for sale—scarcely worn

I can read the future—#1 Yevgeny Street
                    Flat 27B

We never repaid kindness. Or loans of clothes or bedding.

We owned   not
the thinnest goddamn coin.   We moved our feet
that's what we did

and our moving   was what did it.

We could have faced   any
direction
          since what moved us was   the need to move.

We would not sit still. We would not.
We would not ossify.

Not for anything
or anybody.   Instead   we held our course

were calm within it.   We had
our own two feet.   We had the pavement warm
beneath them.   We had each other—pack of pups.

We didn't envy   even God.

{ 5 }

"Lavish, light-fingered, and lilting with wit and imagination, *Casanova* was . . .
a historical fantasia, an epic comedy based on a real-life rogue. For Mosjoukine,
the role of *Casanova* was a pure moment of comic détente. He visibly has a grand
old time sending up the great movieland seducers, himself included . . ."

say the word, *bliss*

when the immaculate night routs
the gaudy sun

& velvet
is
drawn over window after window
& candlelight begins to shine.

(raw morning has yet to be imagined.)

{ 6 }

Michel Strogoff is a movie. I know that.
Mosjoukine isn't Strogoff,
Strogoff isn't real.

Yet, when,
Mosjoukine yells above the panicked rhythm of the horses—

Never be afraid!

I think, *He's talking to me.*
I think, *He knows how terrified I've always been.*

Never mind that he is racing toward
the vanishing of all he knew—
no one could stop the Russian revolution
no one could stop the invention of sync sound.

If he had been more timid, time would still have been the reef
against which all his hopes would break

but in the end, that doesn't matter—
in the end, we all must die
in the end, we all will be forgotten

So take the reins in one clenched hand—
& annihilate

all fear

{ 7 }

As *Kean,* you leave your heartbreak
in the dressing room to play
Hamlet's on the stage instead,
saying, *Actors are not allowed*
their own emotions.

But it seems you spent decades
rehearsing for the moment
when what happened on the screen
became your life as well.

How else to understand
your puzzled sorrow when,
in *Behind the Screen,* you return
from war to find your name
on your dressing room crossed out—
a younger actor's inked in its place.

You wrote the scripts,
or collaborated on them,
directed yourself sometimes as well—
so surely, as you tried on
tragedies for size,
you had at least a premonition
which ones might come true?

& what of all those movies—
The Brigand Brothers,
Kean, Morphia—where,
after squandering great wealth
you die in poverty,

did you ever say, *Ah, so this is deja-vu!*

I do, daily.
I wrote a novel where the heroine
almost dies in childbirth
only to find myself, six years later,
bleeding, bleeding, bleeding
as if dying were the one thing
I had left to do.

Tell me, when you reached
that wretched sanitarium,
did you cry out—
for god's sake, cast another actor,
for god's sake, let me write a better script.

Or did you play *Mosjoukine's Death*
as only

you could do.

{ 8 }

"The rapidity with which [Mosjoukine] is able to shift mood still astonishes, as
does the gift identified by his contemporaries as 'expression in two tones'—the
ability to show the feelings hidden by the expression of an apparently different
emotion."

In *The Late Mattias Pascal,*
for one moment Mosjoukine's grief is boundless

(*I know, I know,* I want to whisper—
I lost a daughter

& a mother too—)

but then his mother's death,
—after agony, after great fear—

& his tiny daughter's

vanish, withdraw
before a battering of water by spiked blue wind
before a brawl from land to sky

he feels a need to ululate, to laugh
he feel a need to turn toward God & bow

though he does neither

only stands

as the enigma
that is life rains down

blunt
absolving
blows

{ 9 }

first,
when we are born
we are not anyone

we are everyone
the way an actor has to be
this is the way
god exists—

then,
because we are not god,
the world
moves slowly in
which is to say, the sun

becomes the sun
the sky,
we learn, is both the sky

& blue

so why a long poem about Mosjoukine?

because he is not me
because he is no one thing

in that, he is like god

as such,
I would not want him for my lover
even
if, as some physicist's believe,
time does not exist—

I do not want to be
his co-star & wife Natalia Lissenko
or Kiki de Montparnasse
or the Polish actress who bore the son
who grew up to be a famous writer
who looked very much like Mosjoukine
who also married actresses
who met an even sadder end

instead, I want to be *be*
Mosjoukine
but without the death from drinking,
the debt, the son I hardly knew.

I want to be Mosjoukine   on the screen
to be *Father Sergius*
& take the axe
to my own finger

if blood is what
it takes
to be that vivid
in a single moment

but on the page—*here. now.*

{ 10 }

Mosjoukine "approached sound films bravely . . . but roles for an actor with
a heavy and ineradicable (and, it was sometimes said, unintelligible) Russian
accent were clearly limited."

Again, night falls—   its whiskers
the prickle of winter

that season
we poets use
as a metaphor for sleep

& death

Such metaphors mean   less than nothing
to me now   Already

I've walked too far
on such thin ice   already

I've said too much . . .

Mosjoukine—
what dialect do you
speak now?

{ II }

Imagine Mosjoukine's life as a silent movie.
Once 18 reels long, now the curators
at George Eastman House have—
in their vast collection—only the last 100 feet,
less than 2 minutes if projected
at the standard 16 frames per second.
In it, Mosjoukine gets married
one last time. The title cards are missing
so it is not clear why the bride is smiling
while Mosjoukine—pale—definitely is not.
Because there is so little left of his life,
we watch it twice. Then—for the hell of it—
the projectionist runs it backwards.
Mosjoukine, trembling, hands back
his ring. The bride goes right on smiling.
They say the Institute of Film in St. Petersburg
may have an alternate ending filmed
for the Slavic market which has always
loved a good cry. In it, Mosjoukine dies—
smiling this time—& misses his own wedding.
Toward the end of Mosjoukine's life,
I fall asleep & dream I'm at his funeral—
nearly the only one who is—but the man
sitting next to me shakes me awake.
Shhhh, he whispers in my ear, no talking
in the movies & no crying, *not real tears.*

{ 12 }

"[In the end,] Strogoff doesn't lose his eyesight to the executioner's burning hot sword . . . because he sheds tears for his poor mother and thus saves his vision. This physiological miracle prepares us for one of the film's great moments: the close-up of Mosjoukine's slowly opening eyes as the villain Ogareff lets out a terrified cry: *He can see!*"

I hope, in the end,

you
could

see clearly

{ 13 }

"[Mosjoukine] died from tuberculosis on 18 January 1939 . . . at the age of 49. He was buried in a poor grave marked only by a wooden cross. Thus . . . his exile continued even in death."

you traveled far & you were rash. the map's crease

turned out to hold deep canyons,

a long sad song of voyage.

the gazetteer, the dead end of the road.

   Be consoled, *old friend*

if existence were balanced on a sword point,

if our crossing were nothing but a burden,

then the map would not be folded,

then there would be no map.

ACT III

Before the Movie

When I think of your small hand, my husband says,
& the sticky warmth of it

I feel jubilant   as if this dim light
were the sun or pair
of them—cardinal & pure

profligate magnified   full of glorious distinction—
all viewed from a distance
like the dead looking up

Fragments from *Le Mogli e le Arance*: Wives and Oranges

"From [writer-director Lucio D'Ambra's] considerable production very little
has survived."

—*Le Giornate del Cinema Muto catalogue*

{ Scene 1. }

[the young marquis
[trembling
[
[the doctor

"two months taking the waters at a spa"

—followed by a silent lecture (on the virtues of an early bedtime?)
intertitle missing

{ 2. }

[the open car
[dust   a long way in the country
[
[a flock of women scatter
[
[turn as one
          [adjust their parasols

—like wings
—a children's story

{ 3. }

[the spa's terrace at breakfast
[flesh by now old   couples, two by two

[

[The noble Baron, who owns the spa:

"Young people need the company
of young people—"
[

[The Baron takes the marquis to his home for lunch
[

[a table lined on both sides with young women

—all with oranges in their laps
—all with hands folded in their laps

         "hope mostly

goes astray   "says the Baron

"but not here, not here"

{ 4. }

—(note to self): *The woman are the daughters of the couples staying
at the spa—but how could each old couple have such a young and
lovely daughter? And why are they staying with the Baron?*

(Partial answer): "I only wish," the Baron says, "there were room
for all of them at my hotel."

—all of them, lovely
—all of them in white

[a face, smiling
[

[folded hands   then again, the oranges
[

[the young people, laughing

{ 5. }

"if not winter,
then no pain   and there is
            no winter here"

—the speaker: an old man (husband of the woman with the little smiling
dog?)

{ Unnumbered—6 or 7? }

["Let me tell you how God made men and women

Oranges, it involved oranges

[cut in two the oranges fell to earth
[each soul a half of what it could be

Love floats all around you. Can't you see it? Wind in the orange trees;
oranges in bloom. Find the one whose half-orange is the perfect mate
of yours . . ."

—The Baron speaking
—The Baron having the last word

{ 8. }

[a game—a dozen women with half oranges
[
—the marquis trying to solve the puzzle by fitting his half-orange to another
[
[first there is a chase

{ 9. }

(time has passed—midsummer?)
—what girl?

52

[oranges rain through his window
[he cannot sleep for oranges falling
—what girl?

—not knowing how he already loves her ankles

[He writes his friends—
            oranges are keeping me awake

{ 10. }

(someone will remember us
            I say
                even in another time—
why else do we make movies?)

—Caterinetta is the youngest
—she will not play the game

{ 11. }

[the friends arrive, stay
[half oranges are fit together, another puzzle solved

—whole oranges   small incandescent suns.

[a shot of old parents—smiling—standing with bride and groom
[a shot of young women walking arm in arm—there are fewer now

{ 12. }

[The marquis leaves
(How much time has passed? Is it always summer?)

{ 13. }

[the Baron finds Caterinetta weeping,
[her orange half in her lap

"*I am too young*," Caterinetta says
"*He would only laugh*"

{ 17? }

(Several scenes are missing)

[The marquis again—the dusty road
[this time, the orange halves fit
—*perfectly*

{ 18. (Caterinetta's age) }

[The Baron in his garden
"God planned it this way, children, never doubt it."

—why else so many oranges?
—why else the parasols?

Le Canard, c. 1925?

"A duck farmer enters into his work with excessive enthusiasm and *amour*."
                                        —*Le Giornate del Cinema Muto catalogue*

We watch as a farmer,
hoeing in a field,

stops work to catch a duck
& fuck it,

wrinkled penis pushing
past the feathers.

The pianist, stunned, stops
mid-note.

The audience falls
more silent than the movie.

The duck, to my extreme surprise,
doesn't seem to mind.

Tusalava

"Tusalava is a Polynesian phrase, inferring that eventually everything is just
the same."

—Len Lye

"Lye always had difficulty explaining what this experimental animated film
was about, beyond describing it as a kind of creation myth, a story from the
Dreamtime. The British Board of Film Censors were not sure what it was about
either, but suspected it might really be about sex."

—Roger Horricks, *Len Lye: A Biography*

I'm in the dark   again. Good.
I like it.

The screen splits.
Black left//   //white right.

Imagine drawing every panel. Lye inked 8 a day.
8=1 second of *Tusalava*. 2 months work for 1 single minute.

Ink pulses, changes into
What?
Grubs? Eggs?

The flashing light would give my friend Allyson an epileptic seizure.
It's giving me a migraine
&
yet—

it is

the tunneled throat of the snake
the blood draining from your body.

Who?   could look away—

Seen from a height

seen through a microscope

seen by mad angels

—this is us.

black pumps into the white until the white is black
then the black sucks the black back into itself

leaving either

great emptiness
or
purity behind.

La Vocation D'André Carel: The Vocation of André Carel

"From his experiences of hard labor working on barges transporting stone, a young man [the son of a famous writer] discovers love, the beauty of the world, and his vocation as an artist."

—*Le Giornate del Cinema Muto catalogue*

In the morning
this land
is a mountain
at night—   it becomes a lake

   It is all a matter of direction

We are on a boat that is carrying
the mountain
stone by stone
across the lake
to build even more Geneva—   what is a city
but cut
stone
set on
stone?

Every week, we sail from our village
built of wood
in a wooden boat

But only after we have loaded each stone
—heavy as a family in our village—
on a wooden barrow
w/ wooden wheels
and rolled it across wooden planks   to stack it upon the deck

In the end—wood pulls
the mountain down, using us
as roots, our fingers pulling,   pulling

as they pull now   at the oars
or the rope   to raise the sail

One day a boy came from the city
to help us with the hauling.

From us, he
learned to work
learned that work is life
earned the love he longed to have

In the end, André married his Reine
daughter of his captain

and with fifty oars we rowed them
the length of Lake Geneva
to their wedding feast—

Then they left us,
for the world   beyond our lake
for a cruise around the world
where they would not   be manning any oars

André, son of his wise father,
took what he had learned of work   of life
He also took Reine
but don't be fooled—   as we were

When André left, he traveled light
and left behind

the stones

L'Hirondelle et la Mesange

"The story was a very simple drama: just a man who, one night, sinks into the [water], and the next day the barge continues on its way, peacefully, in the light and the silence."

—Andre Antoine, the director of the film.

The eye of the river shuts, and then opens, both motions luminous.
Opens, then shuts, both movements dark.

With a double-hooked pole, the captain guides his barge
through the locks of the Loire.

With a double-hooked pole, he holds the mate under the river
until water washes the taste of sweet wine

from his lips. His lips open. The river's
slant eye

shuts, the sand moving like time—that slowly—beneath him.
His bubbled breath parachutes upward.

No matter he was to marry the captain's sister-in-law.
No matter he could sail oceans as well as the river.

He'd planned all along to steal. Now, in a moment, all
is stolen from him.

Halo of light
the valves of his ears blowing open

then water
not in torrents, but ceaselessly, comes unchecked

out of everywhere, drowning
his world.

Germinal

An early adaptation of the Zola novel, "*Germinal* marked the emergence of the industrial landscape in French cinema."

—*Le Giornate del Cinema Muto catalogue*

We remember the darkness; we forget the stars.

Since the mine flooded.
each memory offered back to us by the coal
is darker than darkness,

the dark water winging beneath us
a night flock of starlings.

Already we forget—
was there one sun & one moon
& which one was smaller by half?

We are dying.

But how is that different?
Weren't we born to die, each day
digging our own black-veined grave?

If this mine is not the heaven we counted on
we may get there yet.
Our last breath drifting up
through this coal, through the earth,

a warm wind on the legs of our widows,
the face of striker & owner alike.
Our heat rising like smoke

toward God's communal sky.

Visage D'Enfants

"*Visages D'enfants*, one of the most extraordinary films ever made about children, [reveals] the effects upon a sensitive boy of his mother's death and his father's remarriage."

—*Le Giornate del Cinema Muto catalogue*

Sometimes, *Maman*,
I drape your dress
over the trunk
in the attic & rest
my head in your wool lap.
At night, I dream
your portrait smiles
at me. At your funeral,
I'm ashamed to tell
you, I fainted & Papa
carried me back home.
Pierrette is so little
she's forgetting. I try not
to blame her. Me, every day
I look into the river &
sometimes I hear you
call me. Maman,
I drape your dress
over the trunk
in the attic & rest
my head in your warm lap.
At night, all night,
your portrait smiles.

from the last century

We saw a man in a newsreel
shoot an apple
from his son's shining head—

the *thunk* of an arrow
in a room where many
were laughing

but one woman wept.

D. W. Griffith, December, 1911

"This is the fifth installment of the multi-year retrospective of all available
D. W. Griffith films."

—*The Griffith Project, Volume V*

The translator in her booth
is having trouble—
Billy's Stratagem,
a Griffith short,
came straight from
the *Nederlands Filmmuseum*
with all Dutch intertitles.
What are clearly
pioneers are described,
after a long pause,
as *peasants of new soil.*
Trappers become *peoples*
who make a living
captivating
small, fur-bearing
mammals.

But her translation
is no more strange
than Griffith's Indians.
The same actors who
were dope fiends
and repentant alcoholics
in November's films
now wear wrinkled
skull caps topped
with bristly Mohawks,
wave shiny axes bought

at the local hardware store
as they attack
the settler's fort.

The settlers live.
The Indians don't. The actors
who play them
moving on to Griffith's
next December film,
A Blot on the 'Scutcheon,
where, with an even-handed
splendor, *everybody* dies—
of sword or grief or poison.
God forgot me,
explains the dying heroine,
and I fell. Next to me,
a film scholar falls
asleep, snoring softly.
This is Griffith #388—
we have hundreds
yet to go.

The Acting Career of Charles H. West Considered as Bad Karma

{ 1 }

where is it where is it where is it written that reincarnation is a good thing? *what if what if what if* reincarnation is like the film career of the actor Charlie West? the failure or the weakling in nearly three dozen Griffith films /1909–1912/ each film a new incarnation at the rate of three a month O the cruelty of casting! to be born the jealous miner who almost shoots his brother in *His Mother's Scarf* only to die & be reborn the "evil companion" in *The Crooked Road* who persuades the young husband to choose a life of crime—*never never never* once a rebirth as the hero who saves Blanche Sweet/ Lillian Gish from the brutish invading Yankees in the nick of time

{ 2 }

O Charlie Charlie Charlie I am talking to you now *each day each day each day* did you hope you would *at last* be the one who stood up for truth & right? With each scenario/ each meeting with Mr Griffith/ each day's shooting did hope die a little death along with you? the best you could hope for to fail through weakness of the body—the frail brother who must be sent to a sanitarium in *String of Pearls*—rather than the soul—the good-for-nothing in *For His Son* who gets addicted to the patent soft drink Dopocoke & first steals, then hallucinates & dies—it must have been hard to believe in redemption or cosmic bliss when

{ 3 }

every day every day every day what lay ahead of you was a new role/ new name/ new life in the same old wig where your old sins would visit you in new & fatal ways—where you would ask Mary Pickford shy *Mender of Nets* to marry you only to ruin both your lives by sleeping with an old undeserving girlfriend O O O you must have thought—better to be like Satan an outright villain & say *I choose to rule in Hell rather than serve in Heaven* but your lemur eyes your slight sloping shoulders denied you the role of villain as certainly as hero/ too weak to save the heroine/too weak to murder the one who does/ too weak to walk away so in the *end the end the end* what did you have left? in *The Massacre* your last film of 1912 you are *again* not the one who rescues your wife & wailing helpless infant—someone else gives his life to save them & you arrive to find the two alive through no virtue or sacrifice of yours O how even good luck can become bad karma! is there a god in this vision of the universe we can blaspheme or blame! if there is I imagine you were tempted like Job to curse that god and die—or did mere oblivion began to sing its song so that when D. W. Griffith—himself a god to some—left Biograph to make his greatest movies & didn't take you with him maybe you sighed & sank willingly into the sea of nothingness your acting career becomes—nothing a form of being/ a way of knowing/ a sweet nirvana/ each day a wave/ each week an ocean/ any failure to swim/ nobody's business but your own/

film history as train wreck

{ 1 }

1895
the Lumière Brother's moving picture
of a train arriving at La Ciotat station—

its engine hurtling toward the audience—

makes women faint, men scream,
the crowd stampede for the exits.

{ 2 }

this *may*
or *may not* be true.

critics differ. historians have disagreed.

{ 3 }

the word *cacophony* comes to mind,
the words "burst in uninvited"

but I speak only
for myself

&, honestly, even my mother's mother wasn't there.

{ 4 }

unless she was so frightened after fleeing
from the basement of the Grand Café
she had amnesia

& wandered down the Boulevard des Capucines
along the Canal St-Martin
until my grandfather, keeper
of the Lock of the Barn of the Beautiful,
took pity on this strange girl.

then maybe married her
or maybe not
on that the records disagree.

{ 5 }

so, here is my hypothesis:

a) The men & women *were* scared
& wished, precipitously, to leave.

b) without Auguste & Louis Lumière,
my mother,
& hence me, might not have been invented.

c) this event has already taken place,
in the distant past,

& we can only speculate. we can never *know.*

we can never, like my poor *grandmère,*
be thunderstruck with wonder.

Imagine God as a Camera

"For his film *Napoleon*, director Abel Gance strapped a camera to the chest of
one of his actors, lowered it in a cage into the ocean, lashed it to the back of a
horse. Not until the French New Wave would the camera again come so close to
both actors and action."

—Dan H. Fuller, *On Silent Film*

Imagine God as a camera
at the rich
end of the silent
film era.
The cumbersome
machinery of sound

will come later. For now,
God is as light
as a mouse. He
runs on top of the snow
in Gance's 1927
Napoleon, rides

the boy Bonaparte's sled
as it races down
the frozen slope
during the snowball fight
that foreshadows
all the future emperor's battles.

God swims in the mad sea
as Napoleon flees Corsica
in his inadequate boat,
his sail
the tricolor flag
of the new French Republic.

Swings on a pendulum
over the unclean heads
of the citizens in the Convention
as they in turn cheer
then condemn the Girondists,
Danton, Robespierre.

Follows the hand
of Charlotte Corday
as she raises
her knife above
the turbaned Marat
in his bath.

God as camera
sees clearly
both the guillotine
and the mad clerk
who eats Josephine's
writ of execution,

saving for history
one more empress.
For if a camera
can come *this* close
to death,
surely so can God.

So though fine optics
separate Him
from the beings
He created,
He can almost taste
the ice and blood

in the boy Napoleon's
mouth as a snowball
strikes home,
smell the sweat
of the crowds
welcoming the Terror,

know the sharp
cramp in the heart
Marat feels
as he slips
to God's
side of the lens.

Goodnight Silents

The man beside me is happy to be asleep in his seat.
In the front row, you can stretch out your legs—
the piano rolls in, the lights dim & in five minutes,
you are dreaming your own silent movie. But first,
there is the red velvet plush of your seat to enjoy,
& the moviegoer will sleep here until dawn.
He has already finished his furtive dinner, a *pannini*
& warm beer from the worn briefcase beneath his seat.
A few feet away, the screen rises from the stage:
this close, it is hard to see, it's that big.
At this hour, it's fuzzy even in my eyes. Later,
the projectionist, too, will fiddle & fiddle, trying
to fix fatigue with focus. The moviegoer,
beneath it, stretches further into sleep.

In his dreams, the silence is total, all films
have the delicate hand tinting of early cinema:
blue for moonlight, gold for lamplight, red
for the flames of Mount Vesuvius burning
a model Pompeii to the ashen ground. Shortly,
the house lights will come on. Painful & electric.
One after another, we will stumble into the street,
trying to wake our sleeping feet long enough
to reach our hotels, our waiting, hard Italian pillows,
while the moviegoer sleeps, dreams on. Then—
in just a few hours—we will be back up again.
At that time in the morning, the moviegoer, too,
is just waking. No one has moved him, but
he wakes no stiffer than we horizontal sleepers.
He is heading for the cafe near the *Teatro Zancanaro*
where he takes his morning coffee.

It is a pleasure to walk to the theater this early,
past the moviegoer standing in his cafe, talking
to the young waitress, past the stalls of the weekly
market with their carpet slippers & artichokes
equally well-displayed. Past the grandmothers
in from the country who all smell more strongly
of life & the sweat it takes to keep on living
than any of us sedentary, silent film scholars,
who are freshly showered, though all we did
the day before was sit in our plush chairs
& watch life flicker on the screen before us.
Life as lived in the days of these grandmothers'
mothers. Before there were cars pushing, honking
through the market. Cars to carry their husbands
to Pordenone & bring them back with thinner wallets.
Cars to take their sons off to meet the strange women
who live in even further, distant cities.

Still, in exchange for their sons, at the end
of this year's film festival—or will it be the next?—
they will gain the moviegoer, the one too poor
to bother with hotel rooms, the one who will never
finish his dissertation on D'Ambra's *Two Dreams
with Eyes Wide Open* because his never are,
the one who prefers the cafe just past the theater
to all others: in the end he'll marry that cafe
& the sweet waitress who comes with it & he'll work
from dawn to midnight, on his feet the whole day,
but he'll drink cool beer from his own tap
& leave this life of decaying celluloid behind.

Cars pass during the night, too, but more quietly,
so quietly that, though the cleaners threw the doors
of the theater wide open, the moviegoer
hasn't woken. At night the beams of the headlights,
as they round the curve, reveal the screen,
blank white, waiting for the next day's movies.
Near dawn, they glide cautiously along, you can't hear
a thing except maybe the river & at the edge of town
they disappear into the valley, sinking
in blue shadow—blue for night, green
for nightmares, red for *The End* of silent film.

Keeper of Light

I return to my room & close the tall shutters.
My husband lies down, kisses me
goodnight & I lie beside him.
O that my life may always be this:
An October day in Italy full of movies
& talking about movies & thinking
of what I might write about the day's movies.
The night air outside is cool &
as people pass under the window,
their footsteps ring clear in the night.
I lie in bed, the lamp off, *not reading anything,*
nor thinking of anything but not sleeping,
& I feel light streaming through me as if I
were a single, bright frame of film & outside
there is a calm like a great silent movie,
like God were already sleeping,
like I was   & I am.

Film Upon Film

I will die in Italy in October *on a day I can already remember*.

I will be walking the worn sidewalk toward
the commencement of Le Giornate del Cinema Muto,   the future
a great film I am about to see projected

when a breeze off the river will raise the badge bearing my name
& I will feel familiar hands   lift me
slightly off the pavement, before setting me to one side.

I will die in Italy in October under a hand-tinted sunset

between receiving the program for that year's festival
& the opening night's film at the *Teatre Zancanaro*.
There, on the bridge across the river,   I will fall;

my life a bridge of a white projected over the river
which I will cross with one foot in the films I have seen,
the other keeping pace with the leader   counting down

toward the moment when I will know all things
without having to view them by way of projection.
There,   amid the honking of cars, will suddenly be God

& a bright light rising from the far side of the river like a spotlight.
At the theater, the film will start   without me
the orchestra playing the newly commissioned score—

no one waiting for the entrance of this missing stranger
who is called to a new   destination,
to an opening night of an entirely other sort.

I will die in Italy in October within sight of the *Teatre Zancanaro*

where a great film I will never see is playing.
I will fold   first at the knees
as if in prayer, then at the slightly worn sprockets

of my spine, my vertebrae having had their final run
through the projector of time. When God   calls,
I will not have to stay awake watching any longer,

but will have only to sink slowly down on
the smooth stone of the bridge & kiss the light

before it disappears.   Before I do.

Bang

This is what will happen—
you will step from your cab
& your dog
will be so excited
he will pee
on your new Italian shoes.
Your sister—a woman
with neither pets nor children
who you left
in charge of both—
will weep she's so delighted
you are back
& soon she can go home.
Your three year old
will jump up
to hug you and knock
your glasses off.

This is what you'll hear—
your sister telling you
she mangled the front bumper
on your new car,
your daughter
asking what you brought her,
your son saying
he really really missed you,
the crunching sound
of the family dog eating
your bifocals

& you will wish
you were back in Italy
watching silent movies.
You will have a strong
desire to stick your fingers
in your ears.

Don't. Instead
imagine you are Kate Bruce,
the kindly mother
in nearly every Griffith short.
Smile as only she could—
then open your arms wide
and welcome in
your life.

The Projector

The projector is the only creature alive—
hear it singing in the *Teatro Zancanaro?*
Singing its clacking heart out,
singing its clacking hot electrical heart out just for us—
though we have left it behind.
We who are the projector's greatest admirers,
who make the seconds it counts down—
5, 4, 3, 2, 1 all the way to *fin*—
the rhythm of our lives,
who dream in lively black and lovely white—-
we are flying back to our lives,
our hands falling to our sides
as we sleep heavily or sit restlessly
through the God awful video projections
on our transatlantic flights.
We will be back, we want to sing out—*please wait!*
We alone can hear the tiny fly buzz
of the distant projector.
We alone fret that disaster—broken film, melted acetate—
might arrive before we do,
stop the heart of our beloved.
We will return, we whisper—*wait, wait!*
Our lives spent in passionate silence
in love with that hot light falling on the screen.
So in love, we will scream through the night in aeroplanes
to reach the projector, ready to kiss it
with our dry jet-lagged lips.
So full of love,
our faith has taught us, like magicians, to levitate.
So full of love,
our faith has taught us, like angels, to fly.

Notes

Le Giornate del Cinema Muto, the Pordenone Silent Film Festival, takes place in October in Pordenone, Italy.

The following poems contain opening quotations from *Le Giornate del Cinema Muto catalogue*, 20th edition: *"Kohitsuji*: The Lamb," *"Kurutta Ippeij*: A Page of Madness," *and "Voyage Autour D'Une Etoile."*

The following poems contain opening quotations from *Le Giornate del Cinema Muto catalogue*, 21st edition: *"Ein Werktag,"* "Fragments from *Le Mogli e le Arance*: Wives and Oranges," *"I Due Sogni Ad Occhi Aperti*: Two Dreams with Eyes Wide Open," *"Le Canard, c. 1925?" "Visage D'Enfants,"* and *"La Vocation D'André Carel*: The Vocation of André Carel."

"Mosjoukine in Exile" contains quotations by David Bordwell, Yuri Tsivian, and Lenny Borger from *Le Giornate del Cinema Muto catalogue*, 22nd edition.

The following poems contain opening quotations from *Le Giornate del Cinema Muto catalogue*, 24th edition: *"L'Hirondelle et la Messange"* and *"Germinal."*

The italicized words "on a day I can already remember" in "Film Upon Film" are from "Black Stone Lying Upon a White Stone" by César Vallejo, my translation.

The italicized words in "Keeper of Light" are from *The Keeper of Sheep* by Fernando Pessoa under his heteronyn Alberto Caeiro, translation from the Portuguese by Jonathan Griffin.

Other Books in the Crab Orchard Series in Poetry

Muse
Susan Aizenberg

Lizzie Borden in Love:
Poems in Women's Voices
Julianna Baggott

This Country of Mothers
Julianna Baggott

The Sphere of Birds
Ciaran Berry

White Summer
Joelle Biele

In Search of the Great Dead
Richard Cecil

Twenty First Century Blues
Richard Cecil

Circle
Victoria Chang

Consolation Miracle
Chad Davidson

The Last Predicta
Chad Davidson

Furious Lullaby
Oliver de la Paz

Names above Houses
Oliver de la Paz

The Star-Spangled Banner
Denise Duhamel

Beautiful Trouble
Amy Fleury

Soluble Fish
Mary Jo Firth Gillett

Pelican Tracks
Elton Glaser

Winter Amnesties
Elton Glaser

Always Danger
David Hernandez

Red Clay Suite
Honorée Fanonne Jeffers

Fabulae
Joy Katz

Eavan Boland
Jude Nutter
Robert Bly
— Heather McHugh
Aimee Nezhukumatathil
— Patricia Smith — Blood Dazzler